MILTON KEYNES
A Pictorial History

The *Cock Hotel,* Stony Stratford, the town's premier coaching inn serving travellers on the Holyhead road.

MILTON KEYNES
A Pictorial History

**Dennis Mynard
& Julian Hunt**

Phillimore

1994

Published by
PHILLIMORE & CO. LTD.,
Shopwyke Manor Barn, Chichester, West Sussex
in association with
Buckinghamshire County Library

ISBN 0 85033 940 5

Printed and bound in Great Britain by
BIDDLES LTD.
Guildford, Surrey

List of Illustrations

Frontispiece: The *Cock Hotel*, Stony Stratford

Acknowledgements

The majority of the photographs used in this book are taken from the collection in the County Reference Library in Aylesbury. The collection, which has been built up over the years by donation and by purchase, was augmented in 1992 with the acquisition of all the Buckinghamshire prints accumulated by the postcard publishers Francis Frith & Co. The original negatives to these prints and to Francis Frith photographs of the whole country are preserved at Birmingham Reference Library.

Photographs 2-3, 20-1, 23, 29, 55-6, 60-1, 75, 81, 89, 99, 101, 104, 112, 136, 138 and 153 are from the collection at Milton Keynes Central Library. The photographs numbered 4, 19, 22, 126, 130-2, were purchased by the County Reference Library from the Royal Commission on Historical Monuments (RCHM), whose collection has recently been moved to Swindon.

Thanks are due to the CNT for permission to reproduce illustrations 160, 162 and 170, to Milton Keynes Archaeology Unit for the loan of numbers 52, 119, 129, 133-4, 172-3, to Milton Keynes City Discovery Centre for the loan of number 167 and to Buckinghamshire County Council Planning Department for permission to reproduce numbers 39-40, 154-9, 161, 165 and 168-9.

Mr. J.H. Venn of Great Missenden has made available his own photographs and those of the late Stanley Freese. These are numbered 1, 43, 53, 139-41 and 163-4. The following illustrations come from other private collectors. Sir Philip Duncombe gave permission for the reproduction of item 44, Mr. Peter Kent loaned numbers 143-51, Mr. A.E. Grigg contributed numbers 24, 34-7 and 87, and numbers 26, 32, 50-1, 58, 84, 90-4, 111, 120, 125 and 127-8 are from Dennis Mynard's own collection.

Introduction

Proposals for a new town in north Buckinghamshire were first put forward some 30 years ago, but in 1967 an area of 22,000 acres was designated for its construction. The name of one of the villages in the area, Milton Keynes, was given to the proposed New Town. At the time it was said that the name was chosen because *Milton* was the name of one of England's most famous poets and similarly *Keynes* was that of a famous economist.

The location of the new town in a central position within the country, only an hour's journey north of London on the newly built M1 motorway, was considered ideal by the planners of the day.

Milton Keynes is therefore a new town with a history that spans only the last 27 years. However, the land on which it has been built has a rich and interesting history which is briefly revealed in this book.

Before the development of the city, this part of north Buckinghamshire had little to unify it and the people of the local towns and villages were proud of their individuality. With the development of the city, all of this has changed and the present inhabitants, largely newcomers to the area, consider rightly that they are citizens of Milton Keynes, one of the most successful new towns in the country.

Twenty-five years ago, the early history of the area was virtually unknown. Now, as a result of rescue excavation projects carried out alongside the construction work, the city has a rich historical heritage. There are in fact few parts of the country which have been the subject of such an intensive programme of archaeological excavation, research and landscape recording.

The site chosen for the city lay mainly between the rivers Ouse and Ouzel, south of their confluence at Newport Pagnell. The rivers flowed through gently sloping valleys in a slightly undulating landscape, with heavy boulder clay soils on the higher ground and lighter soils in the valleys.

Early History

Although it is fairly certain that people were active in the area earlier, it was not until *c*.2000 B.C. that people settled here. These first inhabitants lived mainly in the river valleys, and had a simple lifestyle based on the rearing of animals and the cultivation of cereal crops. Several burial sites of this period, dating from *c*.2000 to 1500 B.C., have been found in Milton Keynes. The remains of the earliest known house in the area, a very large circular building some eighteen metres in diameter, dated to *c*.700 B.C., were found at Blue Bridge, Wolverton. This is one of the largest of its kind yet discovered in Britain, and dates from the late Bronze Age or the early Iron Age.

The population of the area gradually increased during the Iron Age and seven substantial settlement sites, ranging in date from 700 to 100 B.C., have been found and excavated.

Some of these were on the heavier clay soils, away from the rivers, confirming that expansion on to more marginal land was required as a result of the increase in population. Throughout this period, the local economy was based on agriculture. The local inhabitants kept substantial herds of cattle, which grazed the riverside meadows, and they also had extensive arable fields on which they grew cereal crops.

Before the Roman invasion in 55 B.C., much of south-eastern Britain was settled by migrants from northern France and the Low Countries. The people of the Milton Keynes area were part of a tribal confederation, the *Catuvellauni*. Their local tribal centre appears to have been a fortified hillfort at Danesborough, one kilometre south-east of the city, the remains of which can be seen in Woburn Woods, near the golf course.

It is interesting to note that the settlement at Bancroft was continuously occupied for 2,000 years, from the late Bronze Age to the early Saxon period, suggesting that this must have been a particularly desirable location. The inhabitants of the settlement there appear to have been extremely wealthy. In the late Iron Age, their cremation burials were accompanied by high quality pottery, jewellery and other items. That this affluence continued after the Roman conquest is confirmed by the building of a substantial Roman-style villa, with under-floor heating, wall paintings and mosaic pavements of high quality, in the nearby valley.

Roman Settlement in the Area

The Romans colonised Britain, constructing an impressive road network throughout the country. One of their main routes, Watling Street, ran through the city area and is now grid road V4. Another Roman road ran from Fenny Stratford to Buckingham and in addition there was a network of minor roads and trackways serving the many villas and farmsteads in the area.

The Romans built our first towns, which became the administrative and market centres for the communities in their surrounding areas. The local Roman town, called *Magiovinium*, covered an area of about seven hectares and was located on the Watling Street, to the south-east of Fenny Stratford. Other Roman settlements in the area varied from small farms at Wood Corner, Woughton and Wymbush to substantial villa establishments at Bancroft and Stantonbury.

The local economy was largely based on agriculture, with cattle or oxen, pigs, sheep, goats, horses and domestic fowl being kept, and extensive cereal cultivation carried out. Local industries included the manufacture of pottery at Caldecotte and Wavendon Gate, iron-working on many sites and bronze-working at Caldecotte. The local population at this time could have been about 3,000 of whom perhaps half may have lived in *Magiovinium*.

Saxon Settlers

Many of the local Roman sites appear to have been abandoned in the fifth or sixth centuries, and it is likely that scrub and woodland grew back over much of the arable land. However, it is most likely that the Saxon peoples who migrated into southern and eastern Britain in the fifth century would have found evidence of extensive settlement and farming when they reached this area. Once here, they soon established large settlements which have been located and excavated at Pennyland and near Milton Keynes village. Chance finds suggest other settlements near Bradwell, Great Linford, Shenley Brook End and several other places. Saxon cemeteries found at Newport Pagnell, Shenley and in Tattenhoe parish have produced burials with weapons, glassware and an iron-bound wooden vessel. The most exciting find was that of a burial with a gold brooch at Shenley.

The Medieval Period

Excavations carried out during the development of the city have shown that the medieval villages were rarely in the same location as the earlier Saxon settlements. The parish system and the villages may have been established as early as the late eighth century, but excavations within the villages have rarely produced evidence to confirm that they existed before the 10th or 11th centuries. One exception is Bradwell village, where excavations on the site of one of the village's manor houses called Bradwell Bury confirmed that it was first occupied in the late ninth century.

The earliest documentary references to the local villages are in the Domesday Survey of 1086. The names of some villages, Shenley ('bright clearing') and Bletchley ('Blaecc's clearing'), suggest that they were probably new developments within wooded areas. This is perhaps further evidence that previously cleared land had become overgrown.

It seems unlikely that Roman or Saxon estate or field boundaries survived to be re-used in the medieval period, except perhaps those that were based on substantial natural features such as rivers, streams and ridges. The Roman Watling Street was used as a parish boundary throughout the area, but it is surprising that none of the villages was actually sited on it.

For administrative purposes parishes were grouped together to form units called hundreds. Most of the parishes in Milton Keynes were in the Saxon hundred of Secklow, apart from those on the east side of the river Ouzel, which were in Moulsoe Hundred, and part of Shenley Brook End which was in Mursley Hundred. Like modern councillors, the men of each hundred met regularly to conduct their administrative and legal business. Unlike

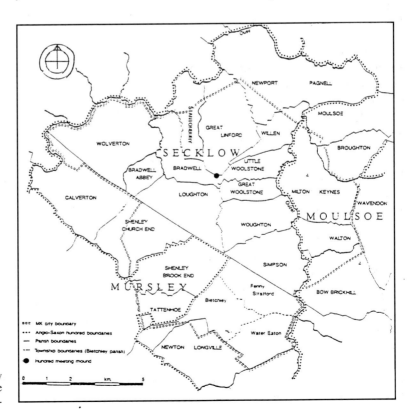

Milton Keynes new city showing the boundaries of the Saxon Hundreds and parishes.

modern councillors they met in the open air at traditional meeting places, often located at a well-known landmark. The meeting place of Secklow Hundred was shown on a Linford Estate map drawn up in 1641 as a slight mound called Selley Hill, situated at a crossroads on the edge of Bradwell and Great Linford.

The mound was the meeting place for Secklow Hundred until the 13th century, when the three hundreds of Secklow, Bunsty and Moulsoe were amalgamated to form the Hundred of Newport. This important mound was located prior to the development of the city centre and has been excavated, reconstructed and scheduled as an Ancient Monument. It can be seen in the public garden at the rear of Milton Keynes Library, only a short distance from its modern counterpart, the Civic Offices of the Borough of Milton Keynes.

In the Middle Ages, the area was well served by roads. The Roman Watling Street remained in use, providing links with the north and south, whilst an important east-west road, linking Cambridge and Bedford with Buckingham and Oxford, ran through the area, linking Newport Pagnell with Stony Stratford. Minor roads ran from the villages to the market towns of Fenny Stratford, Newport Pagnell and Stony Stratford and the name 'Portway' for these roads often occurs in medieval documents. Other roads and minor ways within the area connected the villages with each other and their fields.

North-east of the city area, a road ran from Newport Pagnell through Woburn before joining Watling Street at Hockliffe in Bedfordshire. This important route enabled travellers from London to Northampton and the north to avoid the river crossings at Stony Stratford and Fenny Stratford, the latter often being impassable in winter months.

The only remaining part of a medieval bridge in the area is at Newport Pagnell, where one arch of the North Bridge remains on the south side of the Ouse, in Ousebank gardens. Several other medieval bridges are recorded within the city. One over the Bradwell brook, at the north end of Bradwell parish, said to have been built by the monks of Bradwell Priory, was called 'stonebridge' in the 13th century. Another spanned the Ouse at the north end of Great Linford parish, carrying the road to Little Linford. There were also bridges at both Fenny Stratford and Stony Stratford, crossing the Ouzel and Ouse respectively.

The principal market town in the area was Newport Pagnell which had been established early in the 10th century. Stony Stratford and Fenny Stratford, both situated on Watling Street, were developed as new towns in the late 12th and early 13th centuries, to satisfy the local need for additional markets. The towns were the main focus for the foundation of Guild premises, such as the Guild of St Margaret and St Katherine at Fenny Stratford, part of which can still be seen, and the Guild of St Margaret and St Thomas at Stony Stratford. The latter town was one of the resting places of the funeral cortège of Queen Eleanor, en-route to London, and a cross erected to commemorate this event at the northern end of the High Street was unfortunately destroyed during the Civil War.

Only one medieval manor house survives within the city: this is Manor Farmhouse of late 15th-century date, at Loughton. The moated sites of manor houses can be seen at Great Woolstone, Milton Keynes village, Woughton on the Green and several other villages.

The oldest known surviving domestic building in the city, dating from the early 14th century, is no. 22 Milton Keynes village. This was the bailiff's house on the estate of lord of the manor, Philip de Aylesbury, who resided at the manor house in Bradwell. Until recent years there was a large workshop and timber yard at the rear of this property. Prior to its purchase by Milton Keynes Development Corporation, the estate belonged to the Society of Merchant Venturers.

Most of the older village houses in the city area had timber frames, with panels infilled with wattle and daub or brick, and thatched roofs. Houses in Bradwell, Great Linford and Old Wolverton were more likely to be built with limestone, which was readily available from local quarries.

The city contains the sites of three 12th-century motte and bailey castles: one at Shenley Church End, another at Wolverton and a smaller example at Bradwell. This type of castle was constructed during the dispute between King Stephen and the Empress Matilda. The fact that three castles were erected within a distance of two miles or so of each other is presumably a reflection of the strategic importance of the area. The castle sites survive as overgrown grassy mounds. Their construction is not recorded in any surviving documents and their history is a matter of conjecture. The castle at Shenley was probably constructed by Hugh, Earl of Chester and was in a dominant position, close by Watling Street, an important route at this time. Wolverton was the head of the barony of Wolverton and the castle here would have been held for the King by Baron Meinfelin who was the Sheriff of Bedfordshire and Buckinghamshire in 1125. The small castle at Bradwell is the least well preserved. It may have been built by William Bayeux, who held land here as a tenant of Brian Fitz Count, a personal friend of the Empress Matilda.

North Buckinghamshire had several small religious houses, most of which were founded by c.1200. The only example within Milton Keynes was Bradwell Priory (later Bradwell Abbey) where Benedictine monks were given land by Meinfelin, the baron of Wolverton, to establish a religious house c.1135. Several medieval buildings, including an important pilgrimage chapel, survive at Bradwell, and the monastic fishponds, which can still be seen, are listed in the survey made shortly after the dissolution of the priory.

Most riverside villages had watermills, many of which were listed in the Domesday Survey of 1086, but few of them have survived. One such mill, a timber-framed building, was located and excavated during the construction of Caldecotte Lake. The monks at Bradwell had a watermill near Wolverton which was destroyed c.1840 when the railway viaduct was constructed.

It is a little known fact that Milton Keynes contains the site of the earliest dated windmill in this country to have been excavated. This mill site was excavated at Great Linford and the timber base supports of the mill, made from large oak beams, still survived within the mill mound. Their date, established by radio-carbon dating, confirmed that the mill had been constructed in the first half of the 13th century.

Bradwell had a windmill in the 16th century, but the present stone tower mill, which is the only surviving windmill in the city, was not built until 1815. The construction of this mill is an example of the initiative and enterprise of a local businessman, who took into consideration the proximity of the recently constructed canal, and the Bradwell wharf, in the siting of his mill.

Medieval parks were created by wealthy landowners in order to keep and hunt game. There were several parks in the area and Bletchley Park is on the site of one which was first recorded in the 14th century. The taking of land for the creation of these parks may have resulted in the depopulation of parts of the local villages.

On most manors, the farmers held their arable land in strips scattered over three open fields. In a given year one field would grow wheat, another peas and beans and the third would lie fallow and provide pasture for the cattle. In the late medieval period, some landlords found it more profitable to rear sheep than to grow crops. They enclosed their open fields and many villagers were put out of work and often made homeless. The parishes of Bradwell and Wolverton were partly enclosed by private agreement by the 15th century and Great Linford was enclosed in the mid-17th century. However it was not until the large scale enclosures of the 18th century, each parish requiring a private Act of Parliament to re-allocate its open field land, that the pattern of small fields which survived up to the development of the city was established. These enclosures gave the wealthier farmers large blocks of land on which many built isolated farmsteads at a distance from the village, a common feature of the local landscape before the development of the city.

As a direct result of enclosure, the population of many villages was reduced and they declined. The sites of abandoned houses and roads survive as grass covered humps and bumps. At Great Linford and Wolverton these earthworks were very prominent because the houses had been built of stone, but the remains of the timber-framed houses at Woughton on the Green and Caldecotte were less dramatic. The sites of the former villages at Wolverton and Woughton are both preserved within acres of city parkland.

Turnpike Roads

By the late 17th century, the major roads in the area were all in a poor state and in 1706 the Hockliffe-Stony Stratford Turnpike Trust was established to ensure the maintenance of Watling Street between these two towns. Turnpike trusts were run by local gentry and professional classes who made a genuine attempt to apply the profits from their tollgates to road surfacing, new bridges and wholesale diversions. Turnpike trustees were required to place milestones at the side of the road, giving the distances to London or the nearest large town. These survive on Watling Street, albeit in some places as concrete replacements with newly cast iron plaques. On the Buckingham to Newport Pagnell road, turnpiked in 1815, the milestones were made wholly of cast iron. One of these remains on Stratford Road, west of Wolverton.

The growth of coaching traffic in the 18th century led to a period of great prosperity for Fenny Stratford and particularly Stony Stratford, where the huge coaching inns, the *Cock* and the *Bull*, survive today. These inns had teams of horses ready to take the coaches to the next stage on their journey, and hired out horses to wealthy travellers to pull their own coaches.

The *Universal British Directory* of 1798 enthused over the quality of the inns, and went on, 'The Coventry, Liverpool, Chester and Birmingham coaches pass to and from London through this place every day. Waggons also pass in great numbers almost every day; there are frequently twelve in a week from Manchester only; to set down the names of all those carriers would be only to recapitulate every conveyance from London to Liverpool, Chester etc.'

The Grand Junction Canal

The construction of the Grand Junction Canal between 1793 and 1800 resulted in major changes to the local landscape, cutting many fields in two and creating problems for the farmers, but it also provided work and business opportunities for other local people. Canal-side wharfs were developed at the towns and in most of the parishes through which the canal passed. The largest were at Wolverton, Great Linford and Fenny Stratford. Newport Pagnell was not on the canal, but the town's businessmen formed a canal company and by 1817 a narrow canal was opened between the town and the Grand Junction at Great Linford. The main line of the Grand Junction Canal (now the Grand Union) remains in use to this day, and is a major leisure and recreation facility within the city.

Trade on the canal brought many items to the area including cheap coal and pottery from the Midlands. The canal encouraged the growth of local industries, particularly brickmaking. Many villages had their own brickyards from the 17th century but new brickworks sprang up in the canal-side villages of Little Woolstone and Simpson which had their own brickyards by the middle of the 19th century.

At Great Linford a large brickworks was owned by George Price of Newport Pagnell, and his bricks were transported by canal for the construction of houses in the nearby towns. The site of this yard, which is now a scheduled Ancient Monument, is alongside the canal, where two bottle kilns and the clay pits can be seen. The abandoned clay pits were quite deep until they were partly backfilled by the Newport Pagnell Rural District Council in 1968. The wharfage was destroyed more recently to provide mooring facilities for a boat club.

From 1840-1880 an extensive programme of building was started at Wolverton and New Bradwell to house the railway workers. The Great Linford brickworks were probably the main suppliers of bricks for the construction of Wolverton and New Bradwell, and also for the expansion of Newport Pagnell during the last quarter of the 19th century, bricks being transported along the canal by barge. The demand for bricks resulted in the creation in 1919 of the Bletchley Brick Company, with large brickworks at Bletchley and Newton Longville, which were only recently closed and their tall brick chimneys demolished.

Railways
The coming of the railways to the Milton Keynes area was due to opposition from the Duke of Buckingham to a proposed line through Whitchurch, Winslow, Buckingham and Brackley. The revised route, adopted to satisfy the Duke, ran through Leighton Buzzard, Fenny Stratford and Wolverton. The crossing of the Ouse at Wolverton was a major feat, accomplished by building an embankment nearly three kilometres in length, with a central six-arched viaduct, almost two hundred metres long and twenty metres high.

The opening of the London to Birmingham Railway in 1838 killed the coaching trade overnight. The glamorous coaching inns of Stony Stratford and their more modest counterparts in Fenny Stratford were reduced to sending coaches to meet the trains at the nearest station. Had Wolverton not become a railway centre and created a demand for workers' housing, Stony Stratford would have suffered a greater economic decline, situated as it was in an area already experiencing great agricultural unemployment.

As Wolverton was mid-way between London and Birmingham, it became the point where engines were changed and where passengers broke their journey. The original station soon proved inadequate, and a second, larger structure was also replaced when the main line was diverted to the east of the expanding locomotive and carriage works in 1881. The rapid expansion of this works saw the construction of hundreds of railway workers' houses which were ruthlessly demolished after only 20 years' life when the land was needed for the works itself. Further blocks of railway workers' houses built to the south of Wolverton station were only demolished in the 1960s. The only surviving railway company houses are a row at New Bradwell, restored by the Milton Keynes Development Corporation.

Bletchley also became a railway town as from 1846 it was the junction between the London to Birmingham Railway and a branch to Bedford, and in 1850 another branch from Bletchley to Oxford and Banbury was opened. Bletchley had been a relatively small Buckinghamshire village. The growing settlement around the station began to eclipse the older town of Fenny Stratford and the commercial centre of the parish moved to the west.

The town of Newport Pagnell was not served by the new railway line and again the town's businessmen formed their own company to build a branch line from Wolverton which was opened for goods in 1866 and for passengers a year later. This line ran along part of the former Newport Pagnell canal and the canal basin became the railway goods yard. This branch line closed in 1964 but the route has been preserved and is now part of the city's public footpath/cycleway system.

A major employer in the city area was a printing works, established in 1878 by George McCorquodale, next to the railway works at Wolverton. This firm principally employed the wives and daughters of the railway workers. Although the firm remains in Wolverton, the distinctive brick frontage of the former main works, built in 1884, was pulled down in 1986 in advance of re-development. This frontage and that of the railway works, which ran the length of the town, was a distinctive feature of Wolverton. Much of the wall of the railway works survives and parts of it still carry traces of wartime camouflage painting.

A firm set up by Edward Hayes at Stony Stratford in 1840, to develop and build agricultural machinery, remained in business until 1925. As a result of their success with steam engines, the firm turned to the construction of marine engines, and later complete boats, normally tugs or launches. These were often towed by traction engine to Old Stratford and launched sideways into the canal.

The interest of a local farmer, William Smith, in agricultural improvements led him in 1855 to design and patent a combined double-breasted trench plough and subsoiler, a type of cable-hauled steam plough. In 1861 he held an exhibition of his steam-powered agricultural machinery at Hayes' works. Smith ceased production in 1877, after problems with the newly-formed National Labourers' Agricultural Union, and bricked up one of his ploughs in a barn on his farm at Little Woolstone. It remained there until the 1960s when it was rediscovered and restored by agricultural students in Bedfordshire.

The demand for public transport between Wolverton and Stony Stratford brought about the construction of a narrow-gauge steam tramway between the two towns. The line was opened in 1887 and was extended to Deanshanger in 1888. After many successful years of service, it was closed in 1926, largely as a result of competition from motor buses.

The opening of the M1 motorway in 1959, brought both London and Birmingham within easy reach by car and the area became home to many commuters. The existence of the motorway was one of the major factors which led to the choice of north Buckinghamshire as the site for Milton Keynes.

The new city of Milton Keynes
Post-war Britain looked for radical solutions to the nation's problems. Planners and architects were afforded high status and the task of housing a growing population was given priority. The perception was that London was too large and that its population should be dispersed to new towns. Bletchley, which had accommodated new industry and secret government establishments during the war, sought to expand by taking London overspill population. Under the Town Development Act of 1952, London County Council was able to make agreements with towns like Aylesbury and Bletchley to build their housing estates on condition that a high proportion of the houses would go to Londoners. Over the next two decades, Bletchley Urban District, in partnership with London County Council, developed much of West Bletchley, accommodating about 15,000 newcomers.

Meanwhile, there was a view in Aylesbury that the south of Buckinghamshire was under threat of being absorbed into the London conurbation and that green belt policies alone would not halt the influx of population into the Chilterns. Under County Architect and Planning Officer Fred Pooley, the County Council developed a plan for a new city in north Buckinghamshire to relieve expansionary pressure in the south. It was to be situated north of Bletchley and to accommodate no less than 250,000 people. Whilst the London planners designed garden suburbs for their satellite towns, Pooley envisaged high-density townships linked to a commercial centre by a monorail system.

The plan for a new city appealed to Richard Crossman, Minister of Housing and Local Government in Harold Wilson's first Labour government. The order designating 21,900 acres of north Buckinghamshire as the site for the new city of Milton Keynes was made in January 1967. The newly appointed Milton Keynes Development Corporation built palatial headquarters at Wavendon on the eastern border of the city area. Although the Corporation consulted both county and local authorities, it always had the last word and the monorail city was abandoned in favour of a dispersed pattern of housing within a grid pattern of roads. The subsequent growth of car ownership proved the Corporation's consultants correct and the wide verges on the main roads originally reserved for a tracked transport system were abandoned in later layouts.

During the 1970s, the Development Corporation, with a ready source of government cash, concentrated on building houses to rent. The early grid squares like Netherfield reflected the architects' preference for clean design rather than human scale. When Margaret Thatcher came to power in 1979, she was determined to roll back the power of the state and public housing was a prime target. Milton Keynes Development Corporation quickly moved towards private housing and shared ownership, relying increasingly on sale of assets to fund further development. Later housing areas owe more to the landscape architect and the preference of the householder for privacy and individuality.

Local Government reorganisation in 1974 saw the creation of another strong player in the development of the new city. Milton Keynes Borough Council was formed from the old urban districts of Bletchley, Newport Pagnell and Wolverton and the rural district of Newport Pagnell. The County Council remained in charge of education and social services, but local planning and housing was to be a district function. Milton Keynes Development Corporation was always intended to be wound up when the city was finished and its work continued by elected councillors. Margaret Thatcher merely accelerated this process and the Corporation's assets were transferred to the Commission for New Towns in 1992 with development 75 per cent complete and population at 154,000. The current local government review is expected to make Milton Keynes a unitary authority, independent of the county and inheriting local assets from the Commission for New Towns which is expected to be wound up at the same time.

The success of Milton Keynes in attracting industry and people to a planned environment has confounded the early critics. The city has become a regional office and shopping centre and even those who continue to complain about the amount of investment that was diverted to Milton Keynes are likely to use its facilities and benefit from the pressure for growth which it has taken away from other areas. Although the team that shaped the city was disbanded prematurely, the momentum of development is unstoppable and the population is expected to reach 200,000 around the turn of the century.

1 Bletchley, the southernmost parish within the new city of Milton Keynes, is not mentioned in Domesday Book. It was regarded as part of the manor of Etone, later Water Eaton. The manor house of Water Eaton was taken down about 1560, but the manorial corn mill on the river Ouzel, photographed in 1936, is probably on the site of the mill mentioned in Domesday Book.

2 Water Eaton had a succession of absentee landlords whose agents managed the tenant farms on their behalf. The antiquarian Brown Willis, of Whaddon Hall, was lord of the manor of Water Eaton when this farmhouse was built about 1730. It was converted into a women's hostel in 1974.

3 Another early 18th-century house at Water Eaton, probably built for Brown Willis, is Sycamore Farmhouse. It has now been converted into offices.

4 A later absentee landlord, Philip Duncombe of Great Brickhill, commissioned these estate workers' cottages on Hope Street, Water Eaton about 1830.

5 Simpson is like Water Eaton, bounded on the south east by the river Ouzel, but its longest boundary, on the south west, is on Watling Street. The church and the village centre are, however, located well to the east of the Roman road.

6 The manor house of Simpson was pulled down about 1810. The large house on the left is Simpson House, built for Charles Warren about 1830.

7 This early postcard is captioned Rectory Farm, Simpson. The timber-framed farmhouse is just visible through the trees on the right. The brick cottages survive and are called the Forge but the thatched house on the left has been demolished.

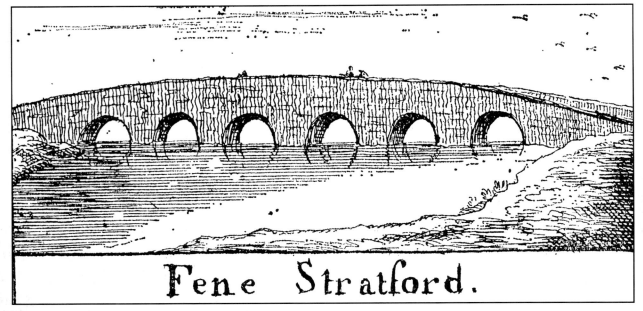

Fene Stratford.

8 Fenny Stratford owes its existence to the bridge carrying Roman Watling Street over the river Ouzel. This 17th-century drawing shows the medieval bridge which crossed the river somewhat downstream from the present bridge. The building of the Grand Junction Canal in 1800 meant that Watling Street had to be raised on an embankment and a new river bridge was required. This bridge was in turn replaced by the present structure in 1935.

9 Watling Street forms the boundary between several Milton Keynes parishes and here in Fenny Stratford the north-east side of the High Street is in Simpson whilst the south-west side is in Bletchley. This 1925 Ordnance Survey map shows the parish boundary diverting from the straight line of the road, following the line of the old road to the site of the medieval bridge and ford.

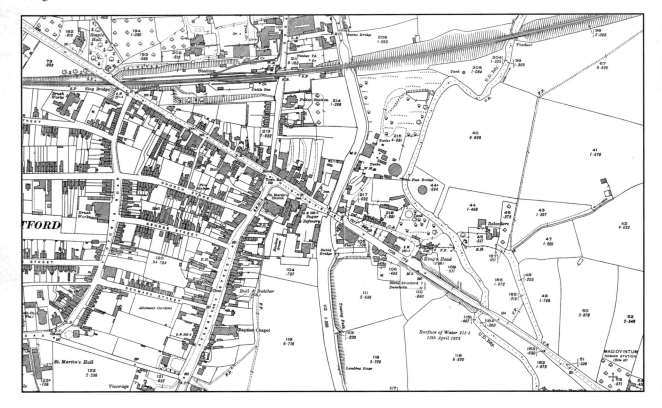

High Street, Fenny Stratford.

10 Fenny Stratford grew up to serve travellers on the road from London to Chester. Although it was not as popular a stopping point as Stony Stratford there were at least fifteen inns and taverns at the peak of the coaching era. The *Bull Inn* was one of the superior kind which catered for the coach passenger and had ample stabling for the post horses. It was completely rebuilt in 1939.

11 The *Swan Inn* on the opposite side of the road was a strong rival to the *Bull* for the coaching trade. The inn was rebuilt in 1878 but the sign on this turn-of-the-century postcard still reads *Swan Hotel and Posting House*, showing that horses had been available for hire to travellers.

12 Fenny Stratford benefited not only from through traffic but also from the road from Aylesbury which joined Watling Street here. Aylesbury Street broadened out at the junction and may have been laid out as a market place at about the time of the 1204 charter giving the town the right to hold a Monday market. This print dates from 1819 and shows a modest covered market in the centre of Aylesbury Street.

A view of Stratf. High Street
att 1715.

A. Ye space between Smyth's & ye Bull
   Barn.
B. Ye Bull Barn.
C. Smyth's houses.
D. Ye Borded Stalls yt are designed to
   be fixt there.
E F. Ye Butcher's shambles.
G. Holme Leigh.

Watling Street.

13   The antiquarian, Brown Willis, who was lord of the manor of Bletchley, 1703-1760, made this drawing of the market place in 1715. He names the building in the centre of Aylesbury Street as the Butchers' Shambles and shows temporary market stalls between the barn to the *Bull Inn* and Watling Street.

14   Next to the *Bull Inn* stands this fine timber-framed building which was probably put up around 1493 when a group of local merchants secured a licence from the king to found The Guild of St Margaret and St Katherine. Such guilds usually had charitable or civic purposes, but the licence enabled the guild to employ a priest to celebrate divine service and to pray for the souls of the members, living and dead. A small chapel would be built which served as a church for the growing hamlet of Fenny Stratford. The chapel was pulled down after the Reformation, but the guildhall was used as a barn, and has now been restored by Milton Keynes Development Corporation.

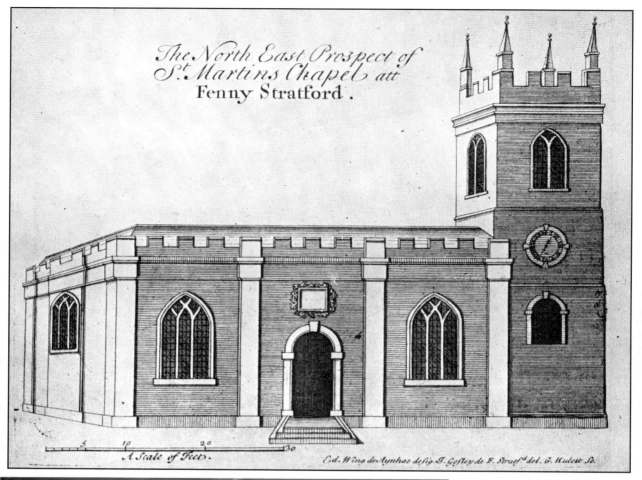

The North East Prospect of
St. Martins Chapel att
Fenny Stratford.

A Scale of Feet.

Ed. Wing de Aynhoe desig. J. Gosley de F. Stratfd del. G. Hulett Sc.

FORTESCU
AND STONOR

15 The people of Fenny Stratford continued to use the church at Bletchley until 1730 when St Martin's church was built, probably on or near the site of the guild chapel. This fine 18th-century church bears comparison with Willen church. It was designed by Edward Wing of Aynhoe in the prevailing classical style, but the promoter, Brown Willis, insisted on the incongruous gothic windows. The 40 ceiling panels are decorated with the coats of arms of Brown Willis and other subscribers.

16 Brown Willis was also responsible for inserting this 17th-century stained glass in the east window of St Martin's, later moved to the present window on the north side. The glass was salvaged from the great house of Sir John Fortescue at Salden near Mursley, which was taken down about 1738.

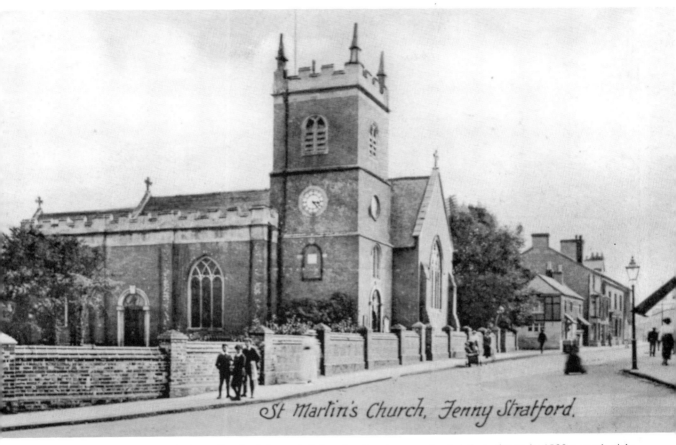

St Martin's Church, Fenny Stratford.

17 The growing population of Fenny Stratford demanded that the church was extended three times; in 1823 a south aisle was added; in 1866 this aisle was demolished and replaced by a new nave and chancel, the original church serving as a north aisle; and in 1907 a new south aisle was added.

18 Aylesbury Street was largely rebuilt in the Victorian period and new residential developments like Church Street and George Street, laid out to the east over land formerly belonging to Home Farm.

19 Home Farm was a large timber-framed farmhouse built in the 17th century. The elaborate shop front dates from 1883. The building had two groups of extremely ornate chimney stacks which were removed in 1928.

20 Further along Aylesbury Street, the Baptist chapel of 1892 contrasted sharply with these thatched cottages which survived into the present century.

21 The Grand Junction Canal, opened to Fenny Stratford in 1800, gave a great boost to the town. This wharf was built to the north of the Watling Street bridge and the former guildhall became part of a prosperous brewery.

22 Inns like the *Red Lion Hotel*, built beside Fenny Stratford lock, capitalised on the canal trade.

23 The London to Birmingham Railway, opened in 1838, destroyed the coaching trade almost overnight. Its loss, which was such a blow to Stony Stratford, affected Fenny Stratford less, as the railway company provided some employment at nearby Bletchley station and Fenny Stratford was provided with a station on the new branch line to Bedford and Cambridge.

24 A Cambridge train at Fenny Stratford in the 1950s.

25 Robert Stephenson's original bridge at Denbigh Hall, carrying the London to Birmingham line over Watling Street, still survives.

26 Beside the railway bridge stood the *Denbigh Hall Inn*, a disreputable inn on this desolate section of Watling Street. The spot achieved brief fame in 1838 when the half-completed London to Birmingham Railway passengers left the train here to travel on to Rugby by coach.

27 As Fenny Stratford expanded, the lane running behind Aylesbury Street was lined with terraced houses and became Victoria Road.

28 With growing numbers of children to educate, Fenny Stratford formed a School Board and in 1890 commenced building the complex of schools now called Knowles First School, where Victoria Road joined the road to Bletchley.

29 The elaborate datestone stands high up on the gable of the former Board School.

30 In 1895 Fenny Stratford Urban District Council was formed to administer the parish of Simpson and the township of Fenny Stratford. Bletchley was added to the Urban District in 1898 and Water Eaton was absorbed in 1934. Council offices were built here at the junction of Victoria Road and Bletchley Road in 1909. In 1911 the name was changed to Bletchley Urban District.

31 The gap between Fenny Stratford and Bletchley was rapidly filled. These Edwardian houses were built at the Fenny Stratford end of Bletchley Road.

Bletchley Rd., Bletchley.

32 At the other end of Bletchley Road, streets of terraced houses were laid out to the north of the road and substantial villas were built along the main road. Many of the larger houses were converted to shops and the concentration of shopping began to move from Fenny Stratford to Bletchley.

33 The transfer of trade from Fenny Stratford to Bletchley continued after the Second World War when Bletchley became the focus of London overspill plans. New factories and council houses were built and the first Londoners arrived in 1952. Bletchley Road was transformed by the building of new shops and the street was renamed Queensway in 1967.

34 In 1846, the village of Bletchley was put on the map by the opening of a station on the London to Birmingham Railway at the point at which a line branched off to Bedford. A branch to Oxford and Banbury was opened in 1850 and the two junctions became the hub of a huge railway complex.

35 The fine station building, with its tall chimneys and Jacobean details was built about 1862 when the branch to Bedford was extended to Cambridge. It was replaced in the 1960s with the present utilitarian building.

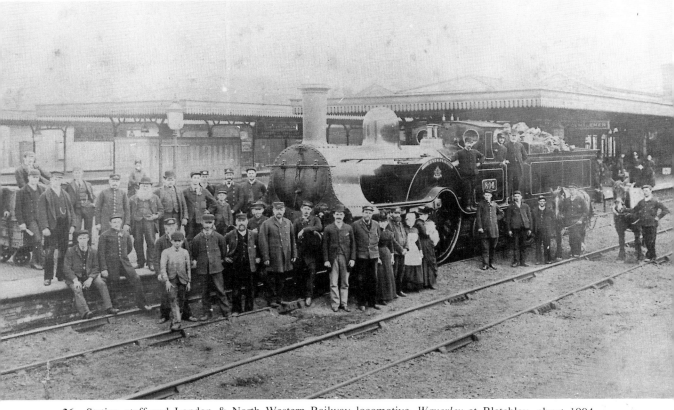

36 Station staff and London & North Western Railway locomotive *Waverley* at Bletchley, about 1904.

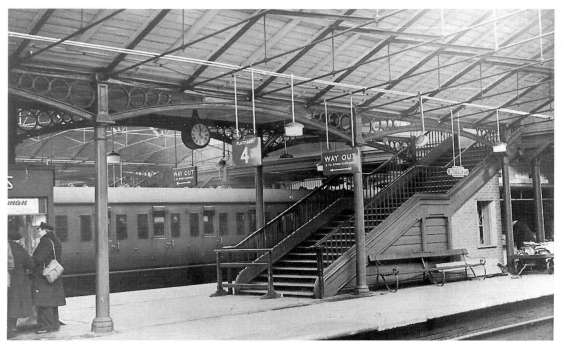

37 Bletchley station about 1950.

38 In the 1950s British Railways planned to build a vast new marshalling yard at Swanbourne, four miles west of Bletchley on the Oxford branch. A concrete viaduct, begun in 1958 and opened in 1962, raised the branch high over the London to Birmingham main line. In the event, the marshalling yard was never built but the viaduct is still in place.

39 Besides the railway, the next biggest employers in Bletchley were the brickworks. The largest of these was the Bletchley Brick Company, actually sited in Newton Longville parish, where the Oxford clay is of a type which contains some combustible elements, enabling bricks to be made with a minimum of fuel to fire them.

40 Bletchley Brick Company was taken over by the London Brick Company in 1929. The brickworks' chimneys could be seen from miles around before the closure of the site in 1990 and the demolition of the last chimneys in 1993.

41 Prior to approval of the plan for a new city of Milton Keynes, Bletchley had agreed to take London overspill population. The first Londoners arrived in 1952, but these houses on Whaddon Way were built in the 1960s as part of the expansion programme partly funded by Greater London Council.

42 The medieval parish church, which had once served Bletchley, Fenny Stratford and Water Eaton, is tucked away to the west of Bietchley station. This engraving was made in 1794.

43 Bletchley church was restored by Brown Willis in 1705-10 and by the Victorians in 1868.

44 Water Hall, the manor house of Bletchley, stood at Water Eaton but was demolished in the Elizabethan period by the Grey family who used some of the materials to build a new house on their estate at Whaddon. Brown Willis, who lived at Whaddon Hall until his death in 1760, nevertheless built a new manor house near Bletchley church in 1710 and gave it the misleading name of Water Hall. This house was knocked down after his death but a drawing by Willis's friend the Rev. William Cole survives.

45 A large house was built in the vicinity of Water Hall by a Mr. Colman in the 1860s. This was bought in 1882 by Herbert Leon, a London financier, who greatly enlarged the house. Leon was Liberal M.P. for North Buckinghamshire 1891-95 and chairman of Bletchley U.D.C. in 1918. The house is best known for its rôle in the Second World War as the base for the code breaking unit called 'Ultra', which was able to decipher German coded messages and to give the government advance notice of enemy plans.

46 Old Bletchley was a typical, if small, Buckinghamshire village of thatched farmhouses and cottages. The villagers tilled their strips in the common fields until enclosure in 1813. This farmhouse is on Church Green Road.

47 Even in Old Bletchley, Victorian and Edwardian villas were being built for better-off members of the new commercial centre growing around Bletchley station.

48 Far Bletchley, the hamlet half a mile to the west of Old Bletchley, remained rural for longer. The *Shoulder of Mutton Inn* is shown on the left where the Buckingham Road crosses the road from Newton Longville to Shenley. The inn was demolished in about 1963 and rebuilt on the opposite corner of the crossroads.

49 From the crossroads at Far Bletchley the road led to the Shenleys and to Loughton. Here the post office and the *Old Swan Inn* were situated.

50 Loughton is the next parish along Watling Street. It was also a typical Buckinghamshire village, with farms grouped around church and manor house and farmland held in strips in three common fields.

51 The Church of All Saints, Loughton is unusual in having a 15th-century south aisle incorporating an earlier south porch, the walls of which have been raised and the whole surmounted by an embattled pediment.

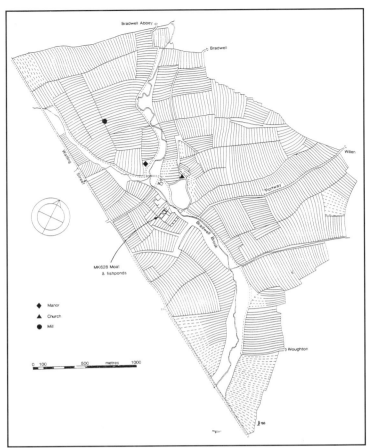

52 Loughton must once have had a large population to feed, as there were no woods and the only land left unploughed was the narrow belt of meadow next to the brook. This map shows the arrangement of the strips of ploughed land before the enclosure of the parish in 1769.

53 Before the enclosure of Loughton in 1769, the land attached to Manor Farm was dispersed in strips around the three common fields. The enclosure commissioners awarded the owner a single block of land to the north west of the Manor Farm, extending right to the parish boundary.

54 Loughton's lengthy boundary on Watling Street must have been a great burden on the parish, which was responsible for repairing this part of the road before it was turnpiked in 1706. From that time turnpike trustees were able to charge travellers tolls to pass their turnpike gates and to apply this money to the repair of the surface. Loughton is shown on this map of the road from London to Holyhead made by John Ogilby in 1675. Regular travellers would have these maps and copies could be inspected at the inns on the route.

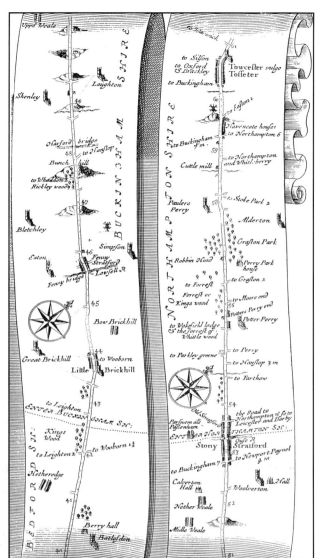

55 Successive turnpike acts required the trustees to erect milestones giving the distances to the principal towns along the road. This milestone stood on the east side of Watling Street just north of Loughton.

56 The *Talbot Inn*, Loughton, is unusual in that it is a purpose-built coaching house with central coach entrance, yet it is not in a town where wealthy travellers might be expected to stop.

57 The *Bell Inn*, Loughton, the three-storey building on the left, was more typical of the wayside inn to be found on Watling Street. It has now been demolished.

58 A fire at a property on London Road, Loughton, brought a photographer to the village in about 1900.

Stony Stratford Bridge.

59 In common with Fenny Stratford, the town of Stony Stratford owes its existence to a river crossing, in this case the bridge over the Ouse. The medieval bridge had three arches plus two culverts to accommodate the regular flooding of the meadowland by the river. Maintaining the bridge was a constant problem for the town and in 1834 one of the arches collapsed as the last wagon in a convoy carrying heavy machinery to Birmingham passed over.

60 The present bridge, comprising three shallow arches, was built in 1835. A toll gate was provided in the centre of the bridge and until 1857 tolls were levied on those crossing.

61 The Buckingham to Newport Pagnell road, turnpiked in 1815, joined Watling Street at Old Stratford in order to cross the Ouse here. The route continued along the Stony Stratford to Wolverton road where this cast-iron milepost is still in place.

62 Stony Stratford is not mentioned in Domesday Book and the regular layout of the building plots on this 1925 Ordnance Survey map suggests that it was the result of deliberate town planning in the medieval period. At this time the parish boundary ran down the centre of the road, the houses on the north east of Watling Street were laid out by the lord of the manor of Wolverton and those on the south-west side by the proprietor of Calverton.

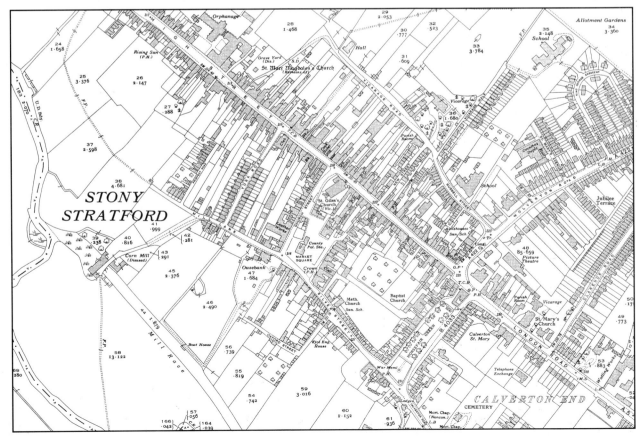

63 The fine corn mill on the Ouse would also have belonged to the lord of Calverton manor. It was regrettably demolished as recently as 1989.

64 It was on the Calverton side that a market place was laid out, probably after 1194 when a market charter was granted. This view of the Market Square dates from 1819 when there remained a rudimentary market hall.

65 The same view a hundred years later shows the police station, built on part of the Market Square in 1864, one of many encroachments where temporary stalls became permanent fixtures and, over the centuries, reduced the size of the Square.

66 This view shows the opposite side of the Market Square with the *Crown Inn* and the elm tree where John Wesley is said to have preached.

67 Before market places were laid out, markets were often held in churchyards. St Giles' church, Stony Stratford, occupies a site between Watling Street and the Market Square, but it is not clear which came first. The medieval church, originally a chapelry under Calverton, was rebuilt in the 1770s, but the tower is from the original building.

68 The present church is built in the 18th-century preaching-house style with galleries on wooden columns, and the roof supported by clustered columns of eight shafts which fan out to form the ribs of the fine vaulted roof.

69 The small chancel in the form of an apse, shown on the left of this photograph of St Giles', was further reduced in depth for road-widening in 1928. The chapel and vestry date from 1892.

70 On the other side of the road is the tower of St Mary's church, destroyed in a great fire which devastated the town in 1742. The church had served the Wolverton side of the town but, after the fire, St Giles' became the only church in Stony Stratford. The tower of St Mary's would have been demolished but for the intervention of the antiquarian, Brown Willis, who (as we have seen), was responsible for the building of the church at Fenny Stratford and the restoration of Bletchley church.

71 On the Calverton side of the Stony Stratford High Street is the *Old George Inn*, a 17th-century building whose ground floor is below the level of the road. The coach entrance to the stable yard at the rear is rather low.

72 On the opposite side of the road is the *Cock Inn*, a magnificent coaching inn dating from the 18th century. It has three storeys, brick fronted with sash windows, with a large archway for the passage of coaches to the stable yard behind.

73 Almost alongside the *Cock* is the *Bull Inn*, built at the beginning of the 19th century, still with its wrought-iron bracket thrusting the inn sign high above the traffic. When sold in 1821, the *Bull* had stabling for 70 horses.

74 The opening of the London to Birmingham Railway in 1838 killed the coaching trade almost overnight, but the construction of railway works at nearby Wolverton created a demand for new houses. Stony Stratford began to expand eastwards to Wolverton and south along the London Road.

75 The new church of Wolverton St Mary was built on London Road in 1863. A vicarage, church schools and a church hall were all built on the same side of the road.

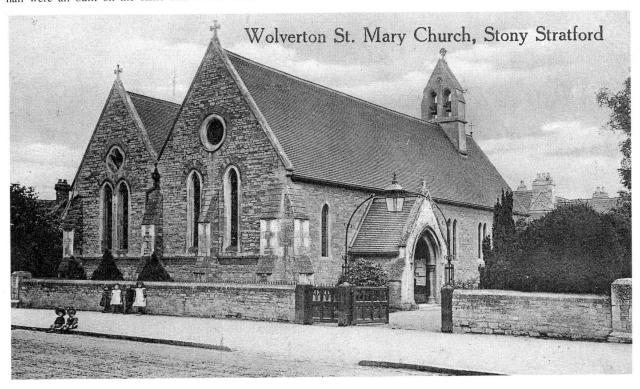

Wolverton St. Mary Church, Stony Stratford

76 The building of the steam tramway from Wolverton to Stony Stratford in 1886 made it easier for the locals to get to work. The tramway was later extended through Old Stratford to Deanshanger.

77 Locomotive no.1 and a car at the Stony Stratford depot. These cars on bogies were unusually large for a narrow-gauge tramway and could accommodate 120 people.

78 Wolverton in 1838 was a village with a population of just over 400. The village had once been much larger and the numerous house platforms visible in the fields near Manor Farm testify to the effects of early enclosure of the village fields.

79 The Wolverton estate had been bought in 1713 by the physician, John Radcliffe, after whom Oxford's hospital is named. Radcliffe left the estate to trustees for the benefit of University College, Oxford.

80 Wolverton Mill was part of the estate administered by the Radcliffe trustees. It still stands at the end of a long mill race parallel to and south of the river Ouse.

81 Stacey Bushes was enclosed by the lord of the manor in the 16th century. A farmhouse was later built at Stacey Hill on what had once been common arable land. The Radcliffe Trustees built the present farm about 1840. It is now the home of the Milton Keynes Museum of Industry and Rural Life.

82 Wolverton's old parish church was rebuilt in 1815 in the then revolutionary neo-Norman style, the funds provided by the Radcliffe trustees.

83 Inside Holy Trinity, Wolverton, the strange rose window is framed by an elaborate Norman-style chancel arch. This photograph shows the fine Victorian wall paintings which were painted over when the church was restored in 1973.

84 (*above*) The Grand Junction Canal cut through Old Wolverton and a wharf was built at the bridge carrying the Newport Pagnell road over the canal. The *Locomotive Inn,* later renamed the *Galleon*, was built to exploit the canal traffic.

85 (*above*) The original line of the Grand Junction Canal which opened in 1800 utilised a series of locks to bring the canal down to the level of the river Ouse. These locks were replaced in 1805 by an embankment and a three-arched brick aqueduct. It was the collapse of this aqueduct in 1808 which led to the construction of the iron aqueduct that survives today.

86 (*left*) The London to Birmingham Railway engineers met the challenge of the Ouse valley with this majestic brick viaduct finished in 1838. It was widened in 1878-82 to accommodate four tracks.

87 As Wolverton was mid-way between London and Birmingham, the railway company built a maintenance and repair depot here, just south of the railway bridge over the Grand Junction Canal.

88 A small station, built to the north of the canal at Wolverton, proved inadequate for the passengers who broke their journey here and a larger station was built to the south in 1840. When the new four-track main line was diverted to the east of the expanding works in 1881, a third station was built, viewed here from the canal.

89 The station building of 1881 was a wooden construction supported on brick arches over the tracks. This local landmark was demolished in 1991.

90 Wolverton Works built locomotives and rolling stock for the London & North Western Railway, but from 1864 locomotive construction was centralised on Crewe whilst Wolverton concentrated on making carriages for the company.

91 The original housing built for the growing workforce was laid out in streets running north to south on the west side of the station. Such was the speed with which the works expanded that most of these houses had to be demolished within 25 years. Only those to the south of the works survived, such as these houses viewed from Creed Street in 1963.

92 Ledsam Street, shown here, was, like Creed Street, named after a director of the London to Birmingham Railway Company.

93 The houses in Ledsam Street may seem dark and cramped, but they would have represented great luxury to the labourer of the 1840s.

94 The railway housing at Wolverton was not built 'back-to-back' as in some of the northern towns. The houses had privies in back yards opening on to an alley at the rear.

95 The style of the railway workers' houses contrasts sharply with that of the Gables, a large house built immediately to the south for the superintendent of the railway works.

96 New housing spread west along Stratford Road in the 1860s. This new street, locally known as the Front, replaced Old Wolverton Road as the main road between Newport Pagnell and Stony Stratford and also became a shopping street for the new town of Wolverton.

97 The steam tramway built in 1886 to bring employees to the works was eventually extended through Stony Stratford as far as Deanshanger. The tram is shown here at Stratford Road, Wolverton.

98 The firm of McCorquodale's had established a strong business in printing for railway companies before they came to Wolverton in 1878. The London & North Western Railway Company were delighted to have the printing works on an adjacent site in order to provide employment for the wives and daughters of railwaymen.

99 McCorquodale's soon won a contract from the Post Office to produce registered envelopes and by 1910 over 500 people were employed in this vast factory between the Stratford Road and the railway works.

100 Church Street, laid out parallel with Stratford Road in the 1860s, also became a shopping street. The tower in the distance is that of the Methodist church.

101 The Wesleyans were the strongest of the non-conformist congregations in Wolverton. Their chapel of 1869 was replaced in 1892 by this large church which had a schoolroom behind.

102 St George's church was built in 1844, remarkably soon after the commencement of the works and the building of workmen's houses. The expense was met by the Radcliffe trustees.

103 As Wolverton's population expanded, the church was extended in 1870 and again in 1895.

104 St George's vicarage was also built in 1844 but the ivy-clad bay window is part of alterations made in 1889.

105 The railway company built a Science and Art Institute on Church Street in 1864. Its style reflected that of mechanics institutes in much larger towns and cities.

106 As early as 1839 the railway company built schools for the children of its employees. The Secondary School was built by the county council in 1906; it was novel, firstly in that it educated a selection of pupils beyond the normal leaving age of 14 and also in that it was co-educational.

107 After the 1944 Education Act the Secondary School became a grammar school and, amalgamating with the Technical Secondary School, became the Radcliffe School in 1958. The school moved to these new premises in 1961.

108 Although Wolverton works reached its peak, employing over 5,000 men before the First World War, Wolverton continued to expand southwards. These spacious houses with large gardens were built on Stacey Avenue in the 1930s.

109 These flats in St George's Way were built about 1962 on the site of the railway works superintendent's house.

NEWPORT ROAD, NEW BRADWELL.

110 The early growth of Wolverton soon presented the railway company with the problem of acquiring more sites for housing. The Radcliffe trustees, who owned most of Wolverton, were reluctant to provide more land. In 1852, land in nearby Bradwell parish was acquired and new houses were built here between Newport Road and the Grand Junction Canal.

111 The new houses at New Bradwell were built in rows running east to west, parallel with the Newport Road. They were bounded on the east by the road to Old Bradwell, otherwise known as Canal Hill.

112 The houses in New Bradwell were built of yellow bricks not seen in this area until the opening of the railway. Two terraces on either side of Spencer Street were restored in the 1970s but the majority of the houses were demolished about 1973.

New Bradwell.

113 The church of St James was opened in 1860 to serve the new settlement. The original design, by G.E. Street, provided for a tower which was never built.

114 (*right*) A large school was built next to the church in 1858, also designed by G.E. Street. It is now a community centre.

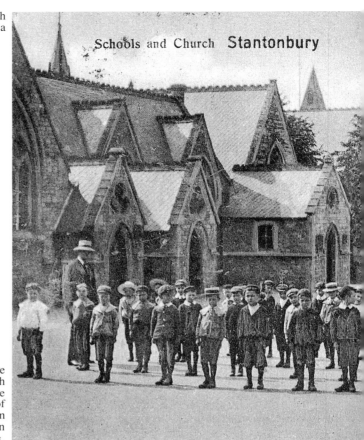

Schools and Church **Stantonbury**

115 (*below*) Stantonbury, the deserted village immediately to the north of Bradwell, had an old church called St Peter's, which served the inhabitants of the new railway houses at Bradwell, until the building of St James'. For this reason, New Bradwell was often known as Stantonbury. St Peter's church collapsed in 1957 after many years of disuse, and is now in ruins.

The Old Church at Stanton Low, Bucks.

116 (*below*) The open pastures of Stantonbury became a place of resort and recreation for the railway workers. This view shows Carr's Mill, an old corn mill on the river Ouse serving the adjoining parish of Haversham.

117 (*above*) New Bradwell continued to expand, and speculative builders added to the stock of railway workers' housing. The inn on the right of this view of Newport Road is the *Morning Star*, demolished in the 1970s.

118 (*right*) The *County Arms*, New Bradwell, was built about 1854 in the bend of the Newport Road known as the 'Corner Pin'.

119 (*above*) In 1867, a branch line from Wolverton to Newport Pagnell was opened, principally to bring employees to the railway works. The last train, shown here at New Bradwell station, ran on 5 September 1964.

120　A Dr. Miles built these houses called 'West View' in New Bradwell in the 1930s. Impressed by the new town of Stevenage, he named two houses on the lane to the windmill as 'Garden City Villas'.

121　These elegant council houses were erected by Wolverton Urban District Council in the 1930s. They were called 'Bradville', recalling Bournville, the garden suburb around the Cadbury factory in Birmingham.

122 Bradwell is best known today for its preserved windmill. Built beside the newly constructed Grand Junction Canal in 1815, it had a working life of only about 70 years.

123 The village of Bradwell is situated about a mile south of New Bradwell. The school, built in 1891, was provided by the London & North Western Railway Company.

e Church, Old Bradwell.

124   The church of St Lawrence, Bradwell, is remarkable for the two Latin inscriptions to be found on the chancel arch. Translated, these are 'Twenty days relaxation' (from what penance we are not told) and 'Dedicated in honour of St. Lawrence' (with an unreadable date).

125 Bradwell House is one of several substantial farmhouses in the village which, prior to the enclosure of 1788, had their land scattered in strips around the two open fields of the parish. It is an 18th-century structure with a 19th-century addition to the east.

126 Bradwell is in an area where stone is more readily available and the older houses are more likely to be of masonry rather than of timber construction. The photograph is of the *Victoria Inn*, Bradwell in 1912.

127 Bradwell Abbey was founded some time after 1154 when the lord of the manor of Wolverton gave part of his land to the monks of Luffield (north of Buckingham) for the establishment of a Benedictine priory. This chapel, which was built against the west wall of the priory church, is the only part of the priory to survive intact.

128 The Abbey Farm has been rebuilt, probably using materials from the demolished priory. In 1971 it was purchased by the Milton Keynes Development Corporation and for many years housed the Milton Keynes Archaeology Unit.

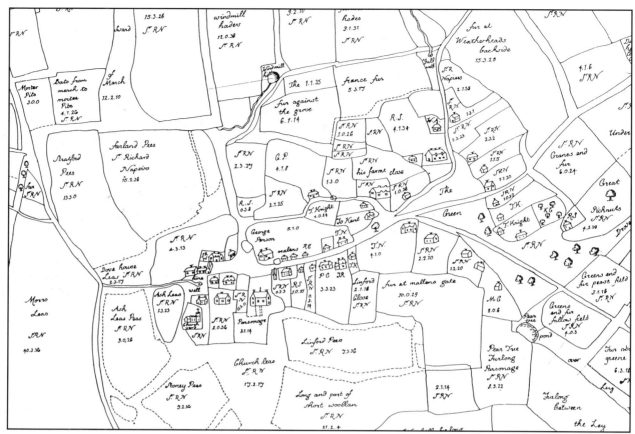

129 Great Linford was transformed by the enclosure of the open fields in 1658 by the lord of the manor, Sir Richard Napier. This estate map of 1641 shows the layout of the village before the enclosure and consequent depopulation.

130 In 1678, Great Linford was sold to Sir William Pritchard, Lord Mayor of London. He built the present Manor House and laid out landscaped gardens which included two pavilions.

131 Pritchard embellished his estate at Great Linford with these fine almshouses with a schoolhouse in the centre. They were built in 1696-8 at a cost to him of £115 15s. 0d.

132 This unusual row of 17th-century cottages stood on the High Street of Great Linford. They were demolished in the 1930s and the occupants were rehoused in council houses built behind the original cottages by Newport Pagnell Rural District Council.

133 These cottages at Linford Green, like those in the High Street, probably date from the enclosure of the village in the 17th century, when many farmhouses disappeared to be replaced by labourers' cottages.

134 With the opening of the Grand Junction Canal in 1799, Great Linford became a distribution centre for a remarkably wide area. The *Wharf Inn* was sited next to the junction of the short branch canal to Newport Pagnell, opened in 1817. The branch was not profitable and was bought by the Newport Pagnell Railway Company as part of the route of their line from Wolverton to Newport Pagnell, which opened in 1867.

135 Another canal-side inn is the *Black Horse*, built beside the bridge taking the Newport Pagnell road over the Grand Junction Canal in the early 19th century.

136 The opening of the Grand Junction Canal encouraged the development of a local brickmaking industry in Great Linford. Cheap coal was available to fire the bricks and it was now practical to transport the bricks over large distances. These brick kilns, on the west side of the canal near Willen Lane, have been preserved.

137 The Manor of Willen was purchased in 1672 by the celebrated Dr. Richard Busby, Master of Westminster School. It was his former pupil, Robert Hooke, a scientist and amateur architect, who designed the new parish church, built in 1679. The old Willen Manor House can be seen in the background on this 18th-century print. It was rebuilt in the early 19th century and is now used as Willen Hospice.

138 Willen church is justly regarded as one of the architectural treasures of Milton Keynes. It was built without a chancel in the preaching-house style, but a chancel in the form of an apse was added in 1861.

139 The river Ouzel, which joins the Ouse at Newport Pagnell, turned the wheels of several water corn mills in the district. Little Woolstone Mill is typical of these smaller mills which were never converted to steam power.

140 Little Woolstone Mill was last operated in 1920. The 10ft.-diameter water wheel is shown here, still in place in 1939.

141 Surely the last water mill to be built in the Milton Keynes area was the small mill erected to the south of Little Woolstone Mill about 1890. Possibly because of a flaw in the design, it was never used to grind corn.

142 The Mill House stood a little way to the south of Little Woolstone Mill. By 1939 it had been abandoned.

143 Milton Keynes village is simply 'Middleton' in Domesday Book. It became Milton Keynes in the 13th century when it was purchased by the Keynes family. Later owners were mostly absentee landlords, not needing a manor house, but the farmhouse shown in this painting, now no.22, Milton Keynes village, dates from the 14th century and could well have been the home of the bailiff.

144 No.22, Milton Keynes village has recently been found to be of cruck construction, each bay of the building being supported by two tree trunks reaching from the base of opposite walls to meet at the apex of the roof. It is the oldest known domestic building in the new city.

145 Behind no.22, Milton Keynes village was a timber yard and workshop.

146 The lord of the manor retained the right to appoint the rector of Milton Keynes. Rectors were usually more prosperous than vicars partly because they were entitled to collect the tithes or tenth of the crops of other farmers in the parish. The rectory was rebuilt in the early 18th century.

147 The lord of the manor owned most of the land and farmhouses in Milton Keynes village, including the Well House, a 17th-century building, now enlarged by the addition of wings at each end. The occupants shown are Mr. and Mrs. James.

148 As agricultural estates like Milton Keynes became more efficient, farms became larger and less numerous. Farmhouses tended to be replaced by farmworkers' cottages, like these superior 19th-century houses.

149 The *Swan Inn* also belonged to the lord of the manor. It is shown here about 1940 with the licensee, Arthur Bird, standing by the door.

150 A National School was built in Milton Keynes in 1859. Most schools in Buckinghamshire villages were, as in this case, promoted by the National Society for the Education of the Poor in the Principles of the Established Church. It is now the community centre.

151 A group of children from very different backgrounds is shown outside Milton Keynes school in 1929.

152 Walton was another small Buckinghamshire village centred on its church and manor house. The old manor house, shown here about 1910, had been down-graded to serve as the home farm. The house in now converted into offices.

153 Walton is best known today as the home of the Open University, established in 1969. The Vice Chancellor's office is in Walton Hall, built in 1830 by the lord of the manor, Charles Pinfold, on a site more suitable for pleasure grounds than the original manor house.

154 The first houses in Milton Keynes were built at a time of shortages, both of building materials and of skilled labour. These system-built houses at Bradville were built in the early 1970s.

155 These aluminium-clad terraced houses were part of a thousand-home scheme built at Netherfield between 1972 and 1977. The roof-line of the blocks was level whilst one-, two- or three-storey homes were sited according to the lie of the land.

156 At Fullers Slade the Development Corporation architects softened the effect of their terraces with Canadian cedar cladding. There were 450 homes to rent in this, the second major housing scheme in the new city.

157 The Fullers Slade development included lots of open space but only tiny gardens in front of the terraces. The photograph dates from 1975.

158 In the 1980s the emphasis changed from houses to rent to houses to buy. In 1981 the Development Corporation promoted 'Homeworld', an exhibition of innovative housing, designed to bring builders and homebuyers to Milton Keynes.

159 Housing development at Bradwell Common began in 1979 including some shared ownership houses. These houses at Wimbledon Place were photographed in 1982.

160 Housing development in the 1980s was on a more human scale. Here at Pennyland, a marina, connected to the Grand Union Canal, provides a landscape feature.

161 Bradwell Village Middle School is typical of many schools in Milton Keynes designed by county council architects in a style they termed 'Bucks vernacular'. Although the country retained selective secondary education elsewhere, Milton Keynes, in the spirit of the 1960s and '70s, was planned so that neighbourhood schools could have close links with the local comprehensive school.

162 A priority in planning Milton Keynes was the disposal of surface water from the newly built-up area which could have made existing flooding in the valleys of the Ouse and Ouzel much worse. The 300-acre Willen Lake, seen here in 1978, was built to take floodwater but has also provided one of the city's major recreational facilities.

163 Most of the major roads in the area of the new city were incorporated into the grid pattern of roads. Watling Street became V4, i.e. the fourth vertical or north-south road. The A5 trunk road has been diverted to the east of the Roman road and is viewed here from a footbridge near the new railway station.

164 An early plan for of Milton Keynes had assumed that townships would be linked to the centre by a monorail system. This idea was dropped and buses, mostly routed along the grid roads, provided public transport. Since deregulation of the buses in the 1980s, smaller vehicles like these have been able to develop more routes within the grid squares.

165 British Rail were cautious about building a new station for Milton Keynes. Central Milton Keynes station did not open until 1982 but it already handles nearly two hundred trains per day.

166 Station Square offices were completed in 1985. The engine on display is a replica of those produced for the London & North Western Railway at Wolverton works in the 1850s.

167   The hub of the new city of Milton Keynes is a commercial centre built at a point where several of the old parishes, including Loughton, Bradwell, Great Linford and the Woolstones, meet. The huge shopping mall, which is the principle attraction for visitors to the city centre, was opened by the Queen in June 1979.

168 It was vital that Milton Keynes attracted sufficient new business to the city to keep pace with the growing population. More than 65,000 jobs have so far been created. These factory units at Blakelands, near the M1 motorway, date from 1976.

169 The plan for Milton Keynes dispersed industry so that people could live near to their work, and there is minimal traffic congestion in the morning and evening. These small factory units at Bradwell Abbey were photographed in 1981.

170 Milton Keynes has become a regional office centre with firms like Abbey National siting their headquarters here. The photograph shows construction in Central Milton Keynes in 1990.

171 Central Milton Keynes gained a landmark when the dome of the new Church of Christ the Cornerstone was lifted into place in December 1990. The church is ecumenical and includes a baptistry.

172 It is appropriate that, only a stone's throw from the present-day centre of Milton Keynes, a pre-Conquest meeting place for the parishes of the district has been preserved. It is shown on this 1641 map of Great Linford as 'Selly Hill'.

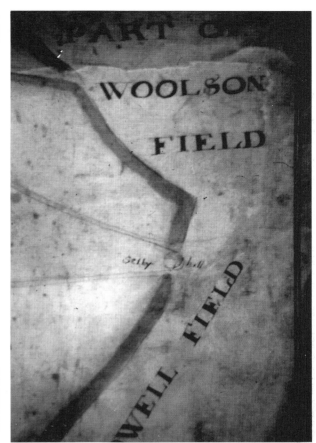

173 Selly Hill, or more properly Secklow Mound, takes its name from Secklow Hundred, a grouping of parishes for administrative and taxation purposes dating from the Saxon period. The mound, which has now been landscaped and incorporated into the gardens behind Milton Keynes Central Library, was the site of the hundredal court for most of the ancient villages around which the new city has been built.

Bibliography

Bendixson, T. & Platt, J., *Milton Keynes: image and reality* 1992

Bradbrooke, W., *History of Fenny Stratford* 1911

Brown, O.F., *Stony Stratford: the town on the road* 1987

Brown, O.F. and Roberts, G.J., *Passenham, the history of a forest village* 1973

Croft, R.A. & Mynard, D., *The changing landscape of Milton Keynes* 1993

Faulkner, A.H., *The Grand Junction Canal* 1972

Grigg, A.E., *Town of trains: Bletchley and the Oxbridge line* 1980

Hassell, J., *A tour of the Grand Junction Canal* 1819

Hyde, F.E. & Markham, F., *A history of Stony Stratford and the immediate vicinity* 1948

Lipscomb, G., *The history and antiquities of the County of Buckingham* 4 vols. 1847

Markham, F., *A history of Milton Keynes and district* 2 vols. 1973-75

Markham, F., *The nineteen hundreds, being the story of the Buckinghamshire towns of Wolverton and Stony Stratford during the years 1900-1911* 1951

Morris, J. (Ed.), *Domesday Book: Buckinghamshire* 1978

Page, W., (Ed.) T*he Victoria History of the County of Buckingham* 4 vols. 1905-27

Ratcliff, O., *History and antiquities of the Newport Pagnell hundreds* 1900

Reed, M., *A History of Buckinghamshire* 1993

Reed, M., *The Buckinghamshire landscape* 1979

Sheahan, J.J., *History and topography of Buckinghamshire* 1862

West, W., *The trainmakers: the story of Wolverton Works* 1982

Whitmore, Colin, *Exploring Milton Keynes* 1990

Woodfield, P., *A guide to the historic buildings of Milton Keynes* 1986

Zeepvat, R., *Roman Milton Keynes* 1991